BOTANICAL SANCTUARIES

Wyoming Ecoregions

- Middle Rockies
- Wyoming Basin
- Wasatch and Uinta Mountains
- Northwestern Great Plains
- High Plains
- Southern Rockies

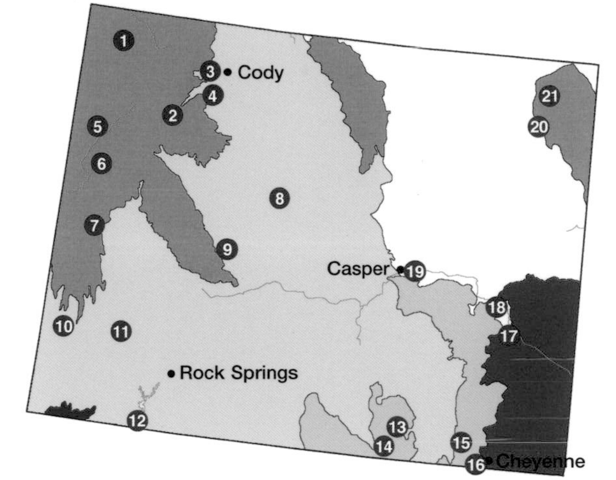

1. Yellowstone National Park
2. Shoshone National Forest
3. Buffalo Bill State Park
4. Pete Miller Park
5. Grand Teton National Park
6. National Elk Refuge
7. Bridger-Teton National Forest
8. Boysen State Park
9. Sinks Canyon State Park
10. Fossil Butte National Monument
11. Seedskadee National Wildlife Refuge
12. Flaming Gorge National Recreation Area
13. Cinnabar Park
14. Flume Creek Park
15. Curt Gowdy State Park
16. Cheyenne Botanic Gardens
17. Guernsey State Park
18. Glendo State Park
19. Audubon Center at Garden Creek
20. Keyhole State Park
21. Devils Tower National Monument

Measurements denote the height of plants unless otherwise indicated. Illustrations are not to scale.

N.B. – Many edible wild plants have poisonous mimics. Never eat a wild plant or fruit unless you are absolutely sure it is safe to do so. The publisher makes no representation or warranties with respect to the accuracy, completeness, correctness or usefulness of this information and specifically disclaims any implied warranties of fitness for a particular purpose. The advice, strategies and/or techniques contained herein may not be suitable for all individuals. The publisher shall not be responsible for any physical harm (up to and including death), loss of profit or other commercial damage. The publisher assumes no liability brought or instituted by individuals or organizations arising out of or relating in any way to the application and/or use of the information, advice and strategies contained herein.

Waterford Press produces reference guides that introduce novices to nature, science, travel and languages. Product information is featured on the website: **www.waterfordpress.com**

Scan for more info

Made in the USA

Text and illustrations © 2009, 2017 by Waterford Press Inc. All rights reserved. Cover images © iStock Photo. Ecoregion map © The National Atlas of the United States.

To order, call 800-434-2555. For permissions, or to share comments, e-mail editor@waterfordpress.com. For information on custom-published products, call 800-434-2555 or e-mail info@waterfordpress.com.

ISBN 978-1-58355-520-0 $7.95 U.S.

9 781583 555200 50795

UPC 8 84682 01152 9

10 9 8 7 6 5 4 3 2 709244

WYOMING TREES & WILDFLOWERS – A Folding Pocket Guide to Familiar Plants

Kavanagh/Leung

T0123990

A POCKET NATURALIST® GUIDE

WYOMING TREES & WILDFLOWERS

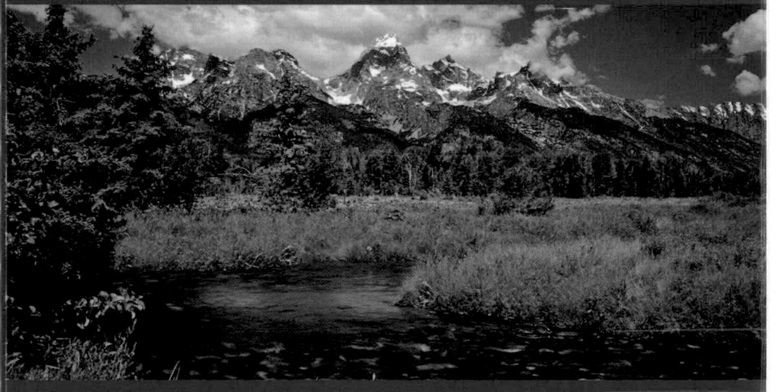

A Folding Pocket Guide to Familiar Plants

TREES & SHRUBS

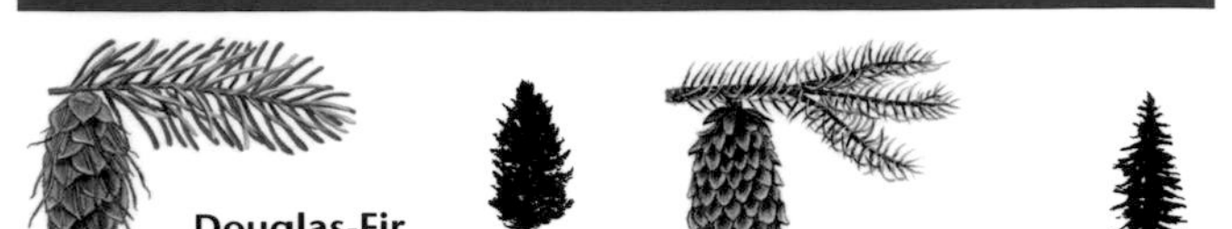

Douglas-Fir
Pseudotsuga menziesii
To 200 ft. (61 m)
Flat needles grow in a spiral around branchlets. Cones have 3-pointed bracts protruding between the scales.

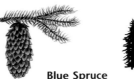

Blue Spruce
Picea pungens To 100 ft. (30 m)
Blue-green needles are up to 1.5 in. (4 cm) long and very prickly. Cones have scales with ragged edges.

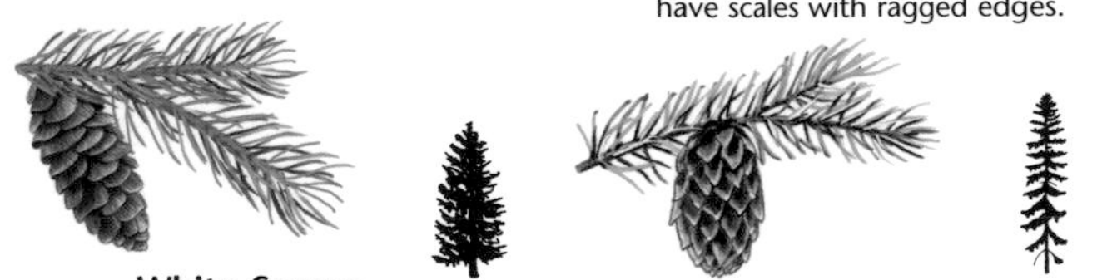

White Spruce
Picea glauca To 75 ft. (23 m)
4-sided, stiff blue-green needles curve upward along branchlets.

Engelmann Spruce
Picea engelmannii To 100 ft. (30 m)
Needles have sharp tips and exude a pungent odor when crushed. Cones often grow in clusters.

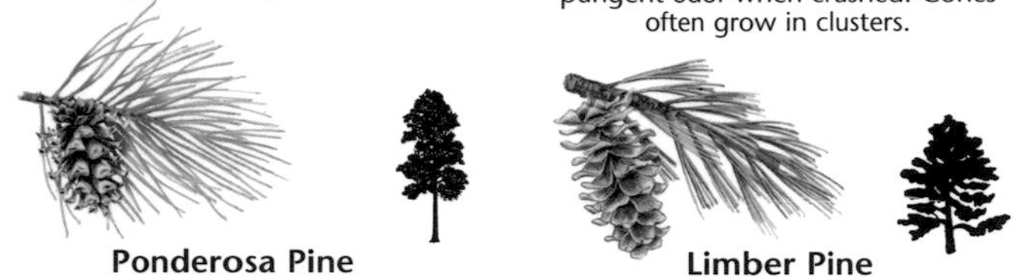

Ponderosa Pine
Pinus ponderosa To 130 ft. (40 m)
Long needles are in bundles of 2 or 3. Cones have scales that have sharp outcurved prickles.

Limber Pine
Pinus flexilis To 50 ft. (15 m)
Needles grow in bundles of 5. Elongate cone has scales thickest at their tips.

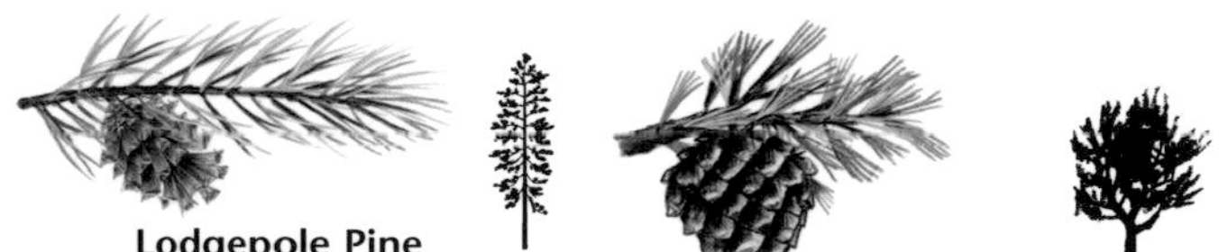

Lodgepole Pine
Pinus contorta To 80 ft. (24 m)
Needles are twisted in bundles of 2. Cone scales have a single prickle near their outer edge.

Whitebark Pine
Pinus albicaulis To 50 ft. (15 m)
Stout needles grow in bundles of 5. Egg-shaped cone has thick scales with sturdy tips.

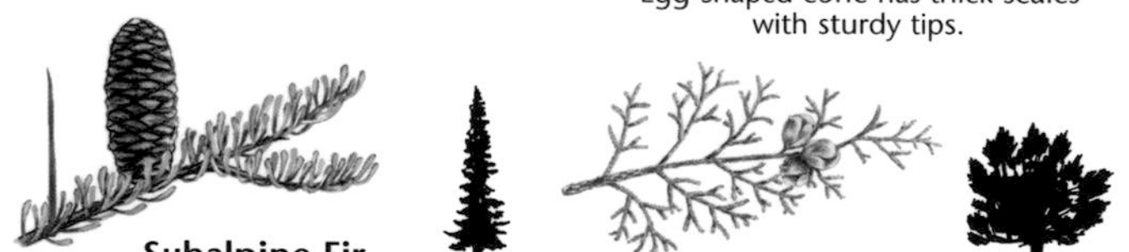

Subalpine Fir
Abies lasiocarpa To 100 ft. (30 m)
Flattened, dark green needles have silvery line on bottom surface. Cylindrical cones grow upright.

Utah Juniper
Juniperus osteosperma To 40 ft. (12 m)
Leaves are small and scale-like. Red-brown, berry-like cones are fibrous.

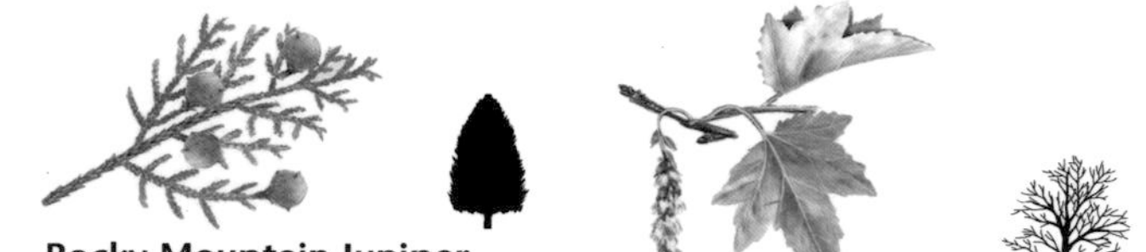

Rocky Mountain Juniper
Juniperus scopulorum
To 50 ft. (15 m)
Has bushy crown of ascending branches. Blue, berry-like fruits have a waxy coating.

White Poplar
Populus alba To 80 ft. (24 m)
Introduced species has distinctive 3-5 lobed, long-stemmed leaves.

TREES & SHRUBS

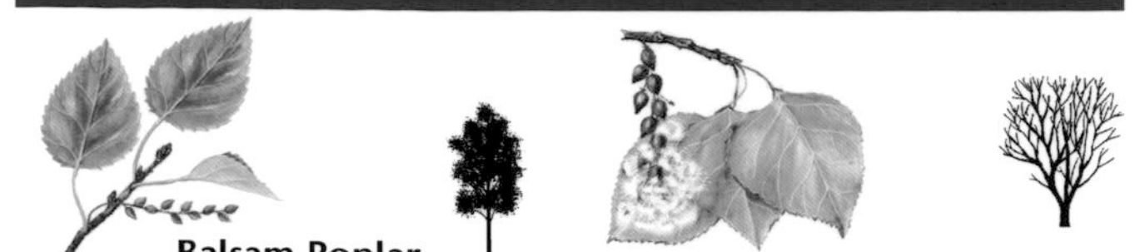

Balsam Poplar
Populus balsamifera
To 80 ft. (24 m)
Drooping flower clusters are succeeded by oval capsules containing cottony seeds.

Plains Cottonwood
Populus sargentii To 100 ft. (30 m)
Leaves are up to 4 in. (10 cm) long. Flowers are succeeded by capsules containing seeds with cottony 'tails'.
Wyoming's state tree.

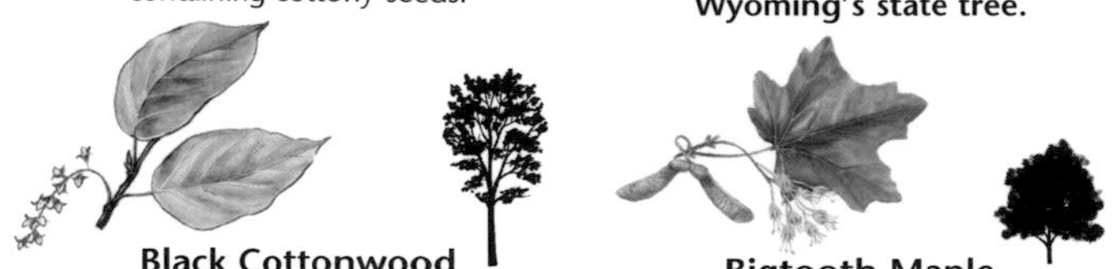

Black Cottonwood
Populus trichocarpa To 120 ft. (36.5 m)
Flower clusters are succeeded by oval capsules containing cottony seeds.

Bigtooth Maple
Acer grandidentatum To 50 ft. (15 m)
Shrub or small tree grows on moist soils. Opposite leaves have 3 main lobes. Fruits are 2-winged samaras.

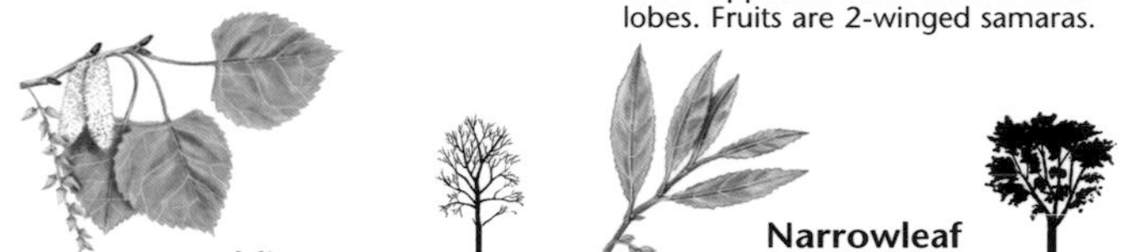

Trembling Aspen
Populus tremuloides To 70 ft. (21 m)
Long-stemmed leaves rustle in the slightest breeze. The most widely distributed tree in North America.

Narrowleaf Cottonwood
Populus angustifolia To 50 ft. (15 m)
Slender tree grows in wet areas. Distinguished by its narrow, lance-shaped leaves.

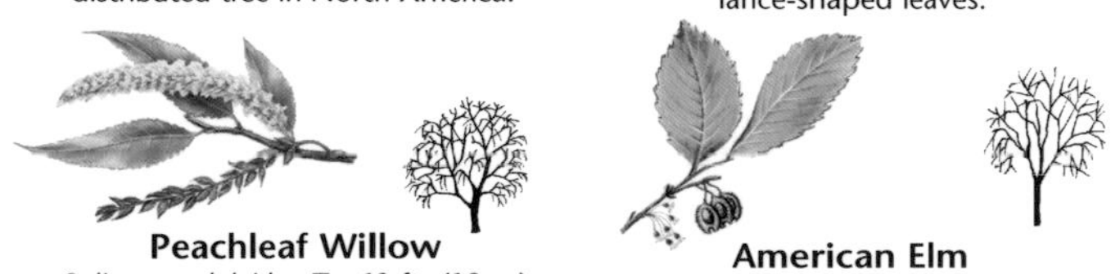

Peachleaf Willow
Salix amygdaloides To 60 ft. (18 m)
Tree has narrow, finely saw-toothed leaves that are hairy below.

American Elm
Ulmus americana To 100 ft. (30 m)
Note vase-shaped profile. Leaves are toothed. Fruits have a papery collar and are notched at the tip.

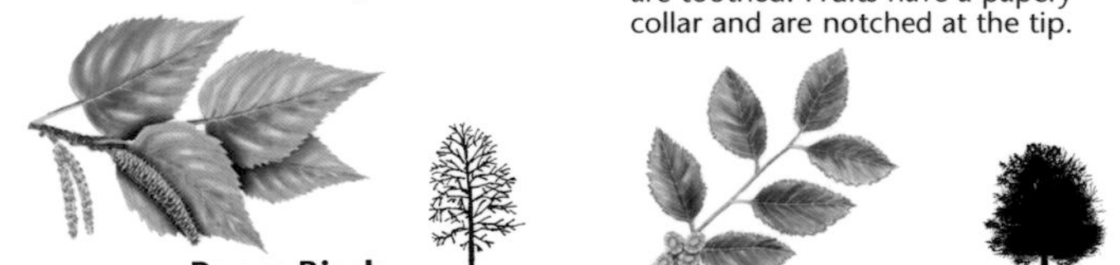

Paper Birch
Betula papyrifera To 70 ft. (21 m)
Whitish bark peels off trunk in thin sheets. Bark was used by Native Americans to make bowls and canoes.

Siberian Elm
Ulmus pumila To 60 ft. (18 m)
Introduced tree has small leaves with short stems. Flowers bloom in drooping clusters of 2-5 and are succeeded by single-winged seeds.

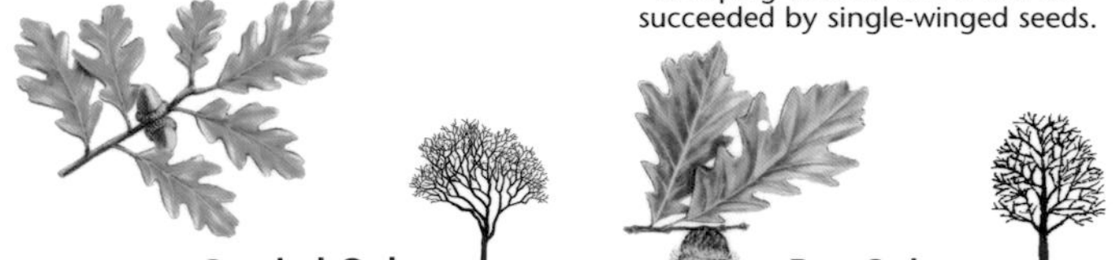

Gambel Oak
Quercus gambelii To 70 ft. (21 m)
Distinctive leaves have 5-9 deep lobes and are to 6 in. (15 cm) long. Acorns are broadly oval.

Bur Oak
Quercus macrocarpa To 80 ft. (24 m)
Leaves have 5-9 lobes and are widest above the middle. The acorn cup is fringed.

TREES & SHRUBS

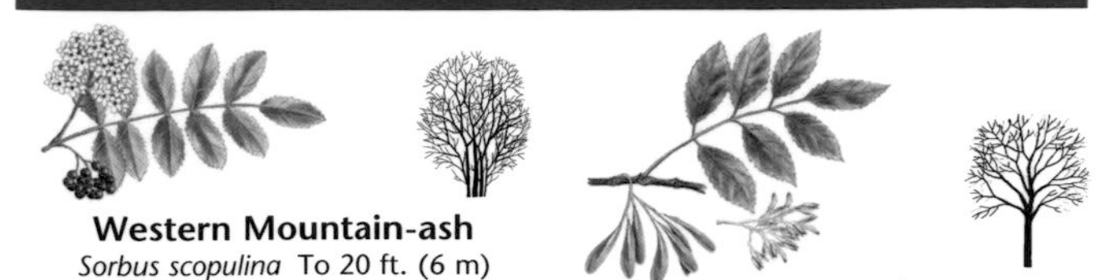

Western Mountain-ash
Sorbus scopulina To 20 ft. (6 m)
Flowers bloom in rounded clusters and are succeeded by clusters of red berries. Common in mountain canyons.

Green Ash
Fraxinus pennsylvanica To 60 ft. (18 m)
Leaves have 7-9 leaflets. Flowers are succeeded by clusters of single-winged fruits.

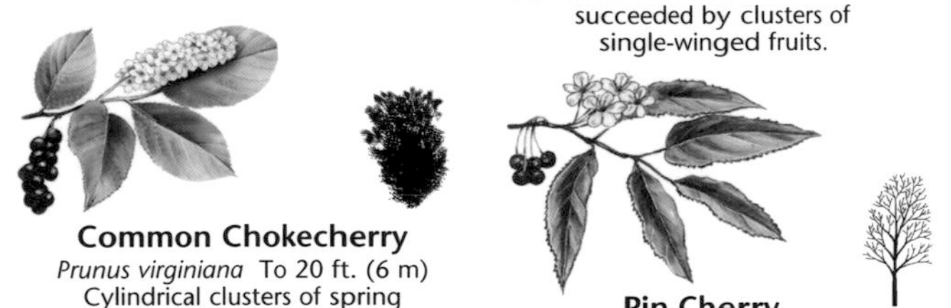

Common Chokecherry
Prunus virginiana To 20 ft. (6 m)
Cylindrical clusters of spring flowers are succeeded by dark, red-purple berries.

Pin Cherry
Prunus pensylvanica To 30 ft. (9 m)
Lance-shaped leaves have curled margins. Small clusters of whitish flowers are succeeded by bright red berries.

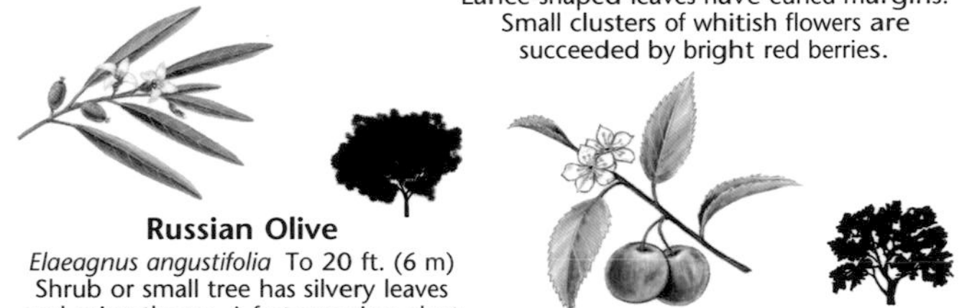

Russian Olive
Elaeagnus angustifolia To 20 ft. (6 m)
Shrub or small tree has silvery leaves and spiny thorns. A fast-growing plant that was widely planted in shelterbelts.

American Plum
Prunus americana To 30 ft. (9 m)
Oval leaves have toothed edges. Bright red fruits have yellow flesh.

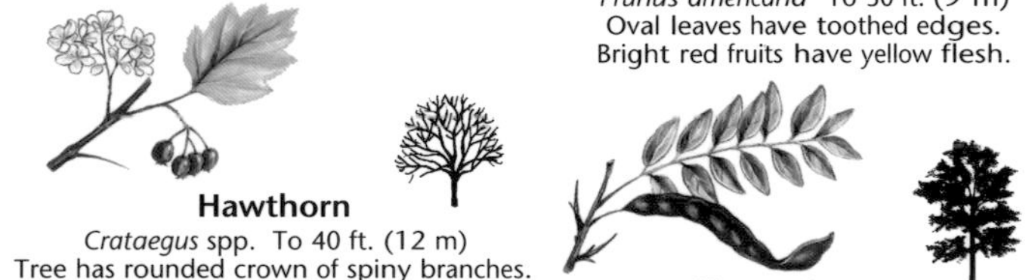

Hawthorn
Crataegus spp. To 40 ft. (12 m)
Tree has rounded crown of spiny branches. Apple-like fruits appear in summer.

Honey Locust
Gleditsia triacanthos To 80 ft. (24 m)
Leaves have 7-15 pairs of leaflets. Twisted fruit pods are up to 16 in. (40 cm) long.

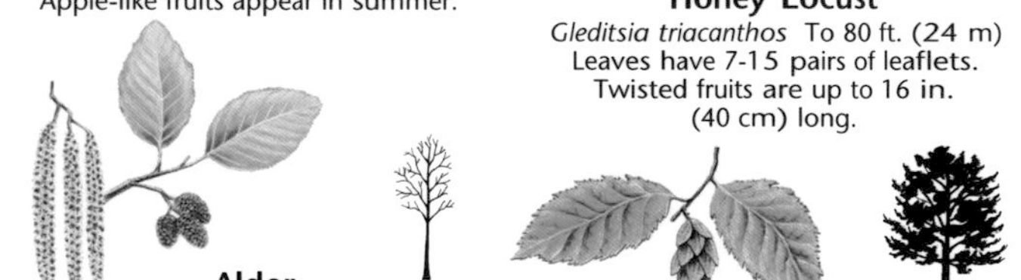

Alder
Alnus spp. To 40 ft. (12 m)
Shrub or tree often forms dense thickets. Flowers bloom in long clusters and are succeeded by distinctive, cone-like woody fruits.

Hophornbeam
Ostrya virginiana To 50 ft. (15 m)
Trunk has sinewy, muscle-like bark. Hop-like fruits are hanging, cone-like clusters. Occurs in NE WY.

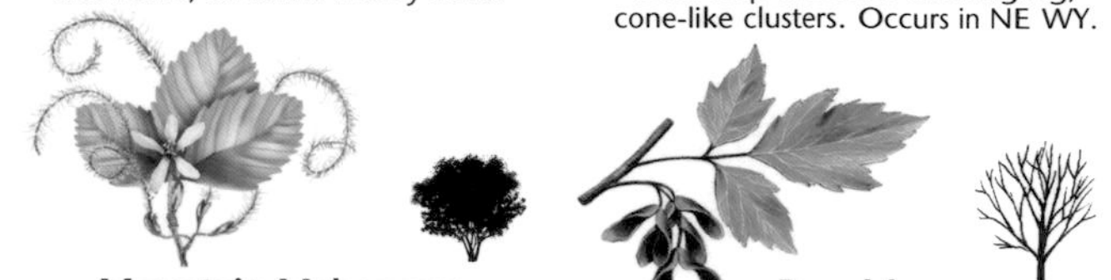

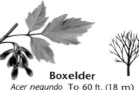

Mountain Mahogany
Cercocarpus spp. To 20 ft. (6 m)
Yellowish flowers are succeeded by fruits with a feathery plume at the tip.

Boxelder
Acer negundo To 60 ft. (18 m)
Leaves have 3-7 leaflets. Seeds are encased in paired papery keys.

SHRUBS & BERRIES

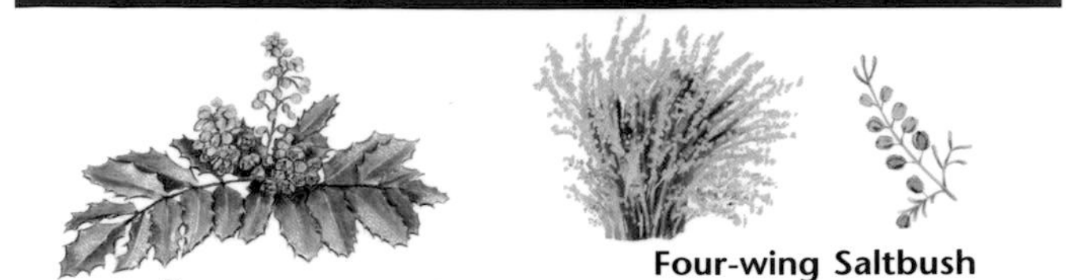

Oregon-grape
Berberis aquifolium To 10 ft. (3 m)
Glossy leaves have 5-7 coarsely-toothed leaflets. Yellow spring flowers are succeeded by blue berries in summer.

Four-wing Saltbush
Atriplex canescens To 6 ft. (1.8 m)
Pale fruits have a 4-winged husk.

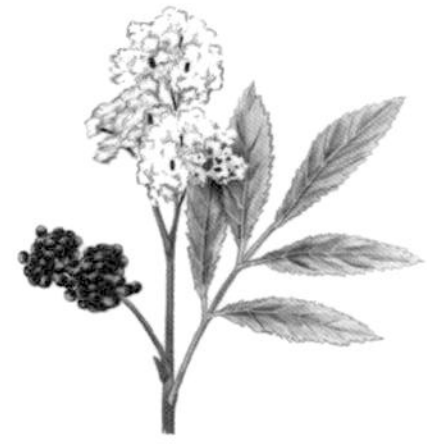

Red Elderberry
Sambucus racemosa
To 16 ft. (4.8 m)
Leaves have 5-7 leaflets and are sharply toothed.

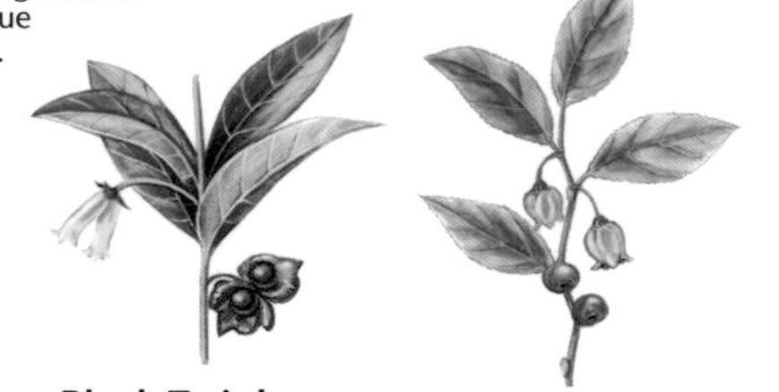

Black Twinberry
Lonicera involucrata
To 10 ft. (3 m)
Purplish, paired berries appear in summer.

Grouse Whortleberry
Vaccinium scoparium
To 12 in. (30 cm)
Carpet-forming shrub.

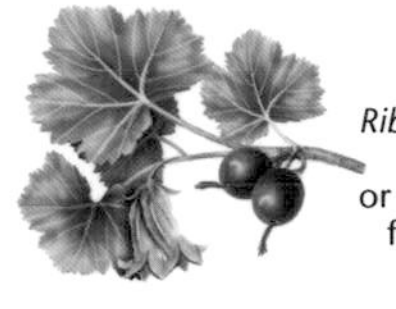

Wax Currant
Ribes cereum To 10 ft. (3 m)
Leaves are kidney- or fan-shaped. White to pink flowers are succeeded by red currants.

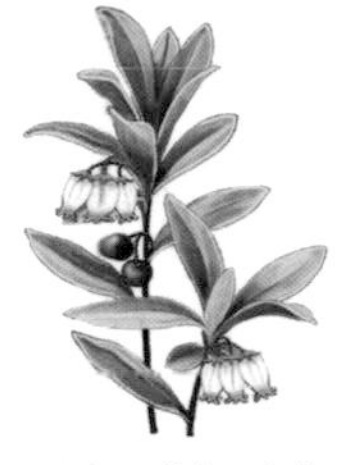

Kinnikinnick
Arctostaphylos uva-ursi
To 12 in. (30 cm)
Pinkish, bell-shaped flowers are succeeded by red-orange, mealy berries. Also known as bearberry.

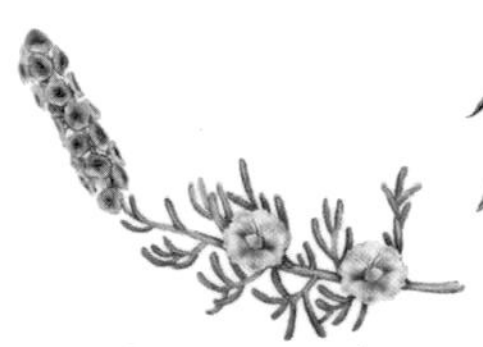

Greasewood
Sarcobatus vermiculatus
To 5 ft. (1.5 m)
Dense shrub has adapted to arid, saline and akaline habitats.

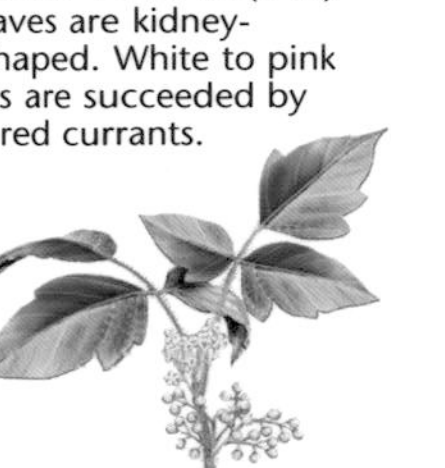

Western Poison Ivy
Toxicodendron rydbergii
To 8 ft. (2.4 m)
Flowers bloom in loose clusters. 3-part leaves turn red in autumn.

GRASSES

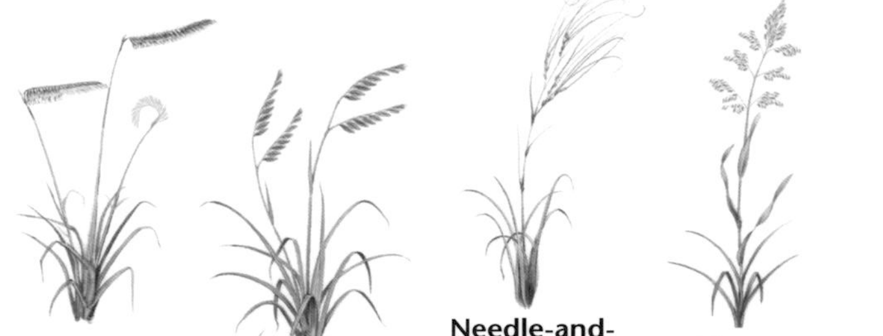

Blue Grama
Bouteloua gracilis
To 20 in. (50 cm)
Seed head looks like short-stalked 'eyebrows'.

Buffalo Grass
Buchloe dactyloides
To 12 in. (30 cm)

Needle-and-thread
Stipa comata
To 10 ft. (3 m)
Needle-like seed looks like a threaded sewing needle.

Bluegrass
Poa spp.
To 3 ft. (90 cm)
Erect stems support pyramidical spikey clusters.

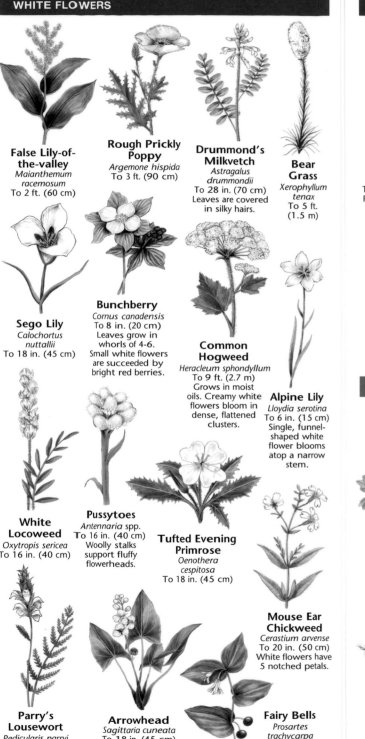

False Lily-of-the-valley
Maianthemum racemosum
To 2 ft. (60 cm)

Rough Prickly Poppy
Argemone hispida
To 3 ft. (90 cm)

Drummond's Milkvetch
Astragalus drummondii
To 28 in. (70 cm)
Leaves are covered in silky hairs.

Bear Grass
Xerophyllum tenax
To 5 ft. (1.5 m)

Sego Lily
Calochortus nuttallii
To 18 in. (45 cm)

Bunchberry
Cornus canadensis
To 8 in. (20 cm)
Leaves grow in whorls of 4-6.
Small white flowers are succeeded by bright red berries.

Common Hogweed
Heracleum sphondyllum
To 9 ft. (2.7 m)
Grows in moist oils. Creamy white flowers bloom in dense, flattened clusters.

Alpine Lily
Lloydia serotina
To 6 in. (15 cm)
Single, funnel-shaped white flower blooms atop a narrow stem.

White Locoweed
Oxytropis sericea
To 16 in. (40 cm)

Pussytoes
Antennaria spp.
To 16 in. (40 cm)
Woolly stalks support fluffy flowerheads.

Tufted Evening Primrose
Oenothera cespitosa
To 18 in. (45 cm)

Mouse Ear Chickweed
Cerastium arvense
To 20 in. (50 cm)
White flowers have 5 notched petals.

Parry's Lousewort
Pedicularis parryi
To 16 in. (40 cm)

Arrowhead
Sagittaria cuneata
To 18 in. (45 cm)
Aquatic plant.

Fairy Bells
Prosartes trachycarpa

Western Bistort
Polygonum bistortoides
To 28 in. (70 cm)
Flowers are white or pinkish.

Twisted Stalk
Streptopus amplexifolius
To 3 ft. (90 cm)
Flowers bloom on bent stems under leaves.

Yucca
Yucca glauca
To 4 ft. (1.2 m)
Large flowers bloom in a long spike.

Canada Violet
Viola canadensis
To 16 in. (40 cm)
White flower petals have yellowish bases that turn violet with age.

Lesser Wintergreen
Pyrola minor
To 8 in. (20 cm)

Globeflower
Trollius albiflorus
To 20 in. (50 cm)

Hooker's Townsendia
Townsendia hookeri
To 3 in. (8 cm)

Western Columbine
Aquilegia formosa
To 3 ft. (90 cm)
Flowers have long spurs.

Heartleaf Arnica
Arnica cordifolia
To 2 ft. (60 cm)
Heart-shaped leaves are sharply-toothed.

Arrowleaf Balsam Root
Balsamorhiza sagittata
To 31 in. (78 cm)
Large leaves are arrow-shaped.

Yellow Coneflower
Ratibida columnifera
To 4 ft. (1.2 m)

Scrambled Eggs
Corydalis aurea
To 2 ft. (60 cm)
Flowers are spurred.

Sulphur-flower Buckwheat
Eriogonum umbellatum
To 12 in. (30 cm)

Yellow Bee Plant
Cleome lutea
To 5 ft. (1.5 m)

Blanketflower
Gaillardia aristata
To 3 ft. (90 cm)

Owlclover
Orthocarpus luteus
To 12 in. (30 cm)

Common St. John's Wort
Hypericum perforatum
To 30 in. (75 cm)
Widespread weed is found in waste areas.

Old Man of the Mountain
Hymenoxys grandiflora
To 12 in. (30 cm)

Plains Prickly Pear
Opuntia polyacantha
Pads to 6 in. (15 cm)
Pads grow in clumps up to 12 ft. (3.6 m) wide.

Glacier Lily
Erythronium grandiflorum
To 12 in. (30 cm)

Yellow Monkeyflower
Mimulus guttatus
To 3 ft. (90 cm)
Flowers are trumpet-shaped.

Blazing Star
Mentzelia laevicaulis
To 5 ft. (1.5 m)
Flower has a central puff of long stamens.

Silverweed
Potentilla anserina
Stems to 6 ft. (1.8 m) long.
Creeping plant. Serrated leaves have 7-25 leaflets.

Alpine Avens
Geum rossii
To 10 in. (25 cm)
Plant has long, feathery basal leaves.

Western Wallflower
Erysimum asperum
To 2 ft. (60 cm)

Shrubby Cinquefoil
Potentilla fruticosa
To 3 ft. (90 cm)
Small shrubby plant has bright yellow, waxy flowers.

Yellow Violet
Viola nuttallii
To 6 in. (15 cm)

Yellow Pond Lily
Nuphar spp.
Flower to 2.5 in. (6 cm) wide.
Floating aquatic plant.

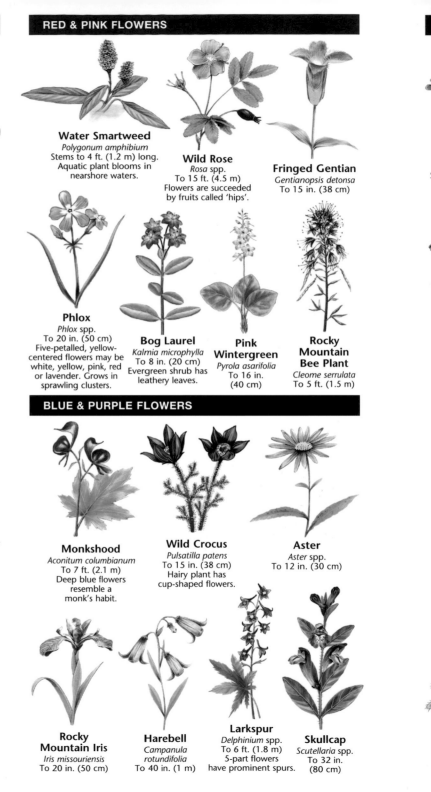

Wyoming Indian Paintbrush
Castilleja linariifolia
To 2 ft. (90 cm)
Wyoming's state flower.

Fairy Slipper
Calypso bulbosa
To 8 in. (20 cm)
Found in damp woods.

Steer's Head
Dicentra uniflora
To 4 in. (10 cm)

Fireweed
Chamerion angustifolium
To 10 ft. (3 m)
Common in open woodlands and waste areas.

Pipsissewa
Chimaphila umbellata
To 12 in. (30 cm)
Waxy, fragrant flowers bloom in nodding clusters.

Pinedrops
Pterospora andromedea
To 3 ft. (90 cm)
Reddish stalk is covered with small yellow flowers.

Shooting Star
Dodecatheon pulchellum
To 2 ft. (60 cm)

Sticky Geranium
Geranium viscosissimum
To 3 ft. (90 cm)
Leaf stems and flower stalks are sticky to the touch.

Skyrocket
Ipomopsis aggregata
To 7 ft. (2.1 m)
Flowers resemble exploded fireworks.

Twinflower
Linnaea borealis
To 4 in. (10 cm)
Flowers bloom in nodding pairs.

Old Man's Whiskers
Geum triflorum
To 16 in. (40 cm)

Dotted Gayfeather
Liatris punctata
To 31 in. (78 cm)

Elephant Heads
Pedicularis groenlandica
To 31 in. (78 cm)
Flowers are shaped like elephant heads.

Moss Campion
Silene acaulis To 3 in. (8 cm)
Mat-forming plant is common above timberline.

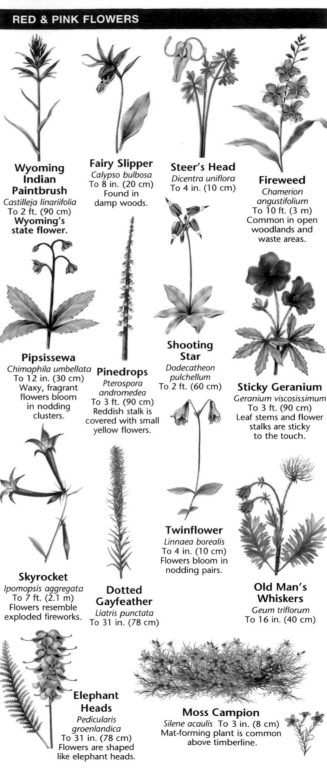

Water Smartweed
Polygonum amphibium
Stems to 4 ft. (1.2 m) long.
Aquatic plant blooms in nearshore waters.

Wild Rose
Rosa spp.
To 15 ft. (4.5 m)
Flowers are succeeded by fruits called 'hips'.

Fringed Gentian
Gentianopsis detonsa
To 15 in. (38 cm)

Phlox
Phlox spp.
To 20 in. (50 cm)
Five-petalled, yellow-centered flowers may be white, yellow, pink, red or lavender. Grows in sprawling clusters.

Bog Laurel
Kalmia microphylla
To 8 in. (20 cm)
Evergreen shrub has leathery leaves.

Pink Wintergreen
Pyrola asarifolia
To 16 in. (40 cm)

Rocky Mountain Bee Plant
Cleome serrulata
To 5 ft. (1.5 m)

Monkshood
Aconitum columbianum
To 7 ft. (2.1 m)
Deep blue flowers resemble a monk's habit.

Wild Crocus
Pulsatilla patens
To 15 in. (38 cm)
Hairy plant has cup-shaped flowers.

Aster
Aster spp.
To 12 in. (30 cm)

Rocky Mountain Iris
Iris missouriensis
To 20 in. (50 cm)

Harebell
Campanula rotundifolia
To 40 in. (1 m)

Larkspur
Delphinium spp.
To 6 ft. (1.8 m)
5-part flowers have prominent spurs.

Skullcap
Scutellaria spp.
To 32 in. (80 cm)

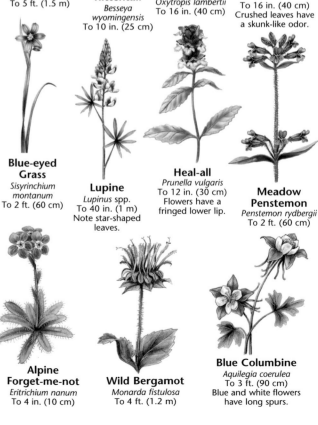
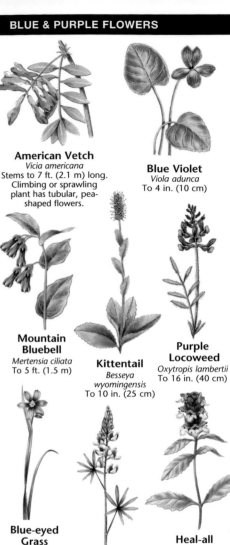

American Vetch
Vicia americana
Stems to 7 ft. (2.1 m) long.
Climbing or sprawling plant has tubular, pea-shaped flowers.

Blue Violet
Viola adunca
To 4 in. (10 cm)

Blue Flax
Linum lewisii
To 24 in. (60 cm)
Stems are wiry.

Mountain Bluebell
Mertensia ciliata
To 5 ft. (1.5 m)

Kittentail
Besseya wyomingensis
To 10 in. (25 cm)

Purple Locoweed
Oxytropis lambertii
To 16 in. (40 cm)

Sky Pilot
Polemonium viscosum
To 16 in. (40 cm)
Crushed leaves have a skunk-like odor.

Blue-eyed Grass
Sisyrinchium montanum
To 2 ft. (60 cm)

Lupine
Lupinus spp.
To 40 in. (1 m)
Note star-shaped leaves.

Heal-all
Prunella vulgaris
To 12 in. (30 cm)
Flowers have a fringed lower lip.

Meadow Penstemon
Penstemon rydbergii
To 2 ft. (60 cm)

Alpine Forget-me-not
Eritrichium nanum
To 4 in. (10 cm)

Wild Bergamot
Monarda fistulosa
To 4 ft. (1.2 m)

Blue Columbine
Aquilegia coerulea
To 3 ft. (90 cm)
Blue and white flowers have long spurs.